A CONTEMPORARY MEDITATION ON PERSONAL HOLINESS

A CONTEMPORARY MEDITATION ON PERSONAL HOLINESS

by TIMOTHY E. O'CONNELL

THE THOMAS MORE PRESS

All Scriptural citations are taken from
*The Holy Bible, Revised Standard Version,
Catholic Edition.* Camden, N.J.: Thomas
Nelson & Sons, 1965.

ISBN: 0-88347-059-4

D.H.O'C.

CONTENTS

Chapter One

PERSONAL HOLINESS

"I was walking along the beach," said my friend, "when suddenly I came upon one of the most beautiful birds I had ever seen. It was not large, but it was exquisitely colored in yellows and oranges. And it moved with consummate grace. It didn't strain with wild flapping; it glided, gently, effortlessly. Riding on the back seat of the wind.

"And then I caught myself thinking. Wondering what sort of bird this was, what name it had, what species it belonged to. And I became very, very depressed. Why did I have to analyze that poor bird? Why couldn't I just enjoy it, just contemplate its nameless beauty? Why did I have to label it? Why did I have to define it?"

My friend's question has always remained with me. And I have never been able to answer it. I know what he is talking about. I know that man's

9

passion for definition can sterilize and eviscerate his experience. I know that life is more important than labels, that appreciation is more rewarding than analysis.

But I also know that we must have both.

Sooner or later in every experience, in every conversation, a simple question occurs: "What are you talking about?" And that question will not be repressed, its challenge cannot be ignored. A definition is demanded, and it must be supplied.

Thus, if at the very outset of these meditations I hear myself asking what personal holiness is, I am embarrassed but not apologetic. Whether I like it or not, I must tell myself what I am talking about. And if you and I are to communicate at all in the course of these meditations, I must invite you into my world. I must share with you the starting point for my reflections. I must give you a definition.

What, then, is personal holiness? Some people have suggested that "holiness is wholeness," that it is the total integration of the person, in touch with himself, his world, and his God. And that definition has much to commend it. Certainly holiness ought to be wholeness. All other things being equal, a man's spirituality ought to resonate freely through the levels of his person. And contrariwise, personal growth in maturity ought to result in a true spirit of holiness.

But all things rarely are equal. And that's the rub. Man is simply too complex for such a clear-cut comparison. Mental illness cannot always be prayed away. And neurosis, like an unwanted guest, sometimes remains even when it is asked to leave. For a whole complex of reasons, then, wholeness and health may not be within the grasp of a particular person. But is this to say that holiness is denied him, too? I think not. The human personality has many levels, and sanctity at one level can surely co-exist with sickness at another.

The most that can be said, then, is that there is a certain degree of co-relation between holiness and wholeness and that *ideally* the two should be identified. But whether they are or can be identified in each Christian person remains an open question.

So what is personal holiness? Is it perhaps piety, a certain reverential spirit in one's life? This definition, too, has a certain plausibility to it, a certain appeal. But I think that it, also, is ultimately inadequate. Certainly if by piety we mean the external trappings of prayer and penance, we are far from the mark. A "saintly" posture, with folded hands and downcast eyes, can equally well be a ruse or an exercise in self-deception. And even if it is authentic, it is at most the fruit of personal holiness and not its definition.

But what of inner piety? Once again, I think the answer is the same. An inner spirit of quiet reverence is surely a value. But only insofar as it springs forth from the font of genuine holiness. Personal holiness precedes piety, and is the root from which piety grows.

So we are still left with our question. What is personal holiness? I believe that when all is said and done the simplest definition may be the best. Personal holiness is the reality of union with God.

It is not some action of our own, nor the result of such an action. It is not any particular manifestation, any set of characteristics. And it is not a goal, though it may be *our* goal. No, it is simply a reality, a fact. It either exists or it does not.

And it is the fact of union. It is not so much a quality of the individual person as it is the connection between that person and his God. It is the profound and penetrating oneness of those two. Just as chemical elements are bonded together to form a compound, so the Christian person and God are bonded together to form personal holiness.

That, then, is the definition I prefer, the definition I will presuppose throughout these meditations. And it is a simple definition, indeed. But if it is simple, it is nevertheless far-reaching in its implications. So perhaps we should make this definition itself the first topic for our meditation. Perhaps before we conclude this chapter we should try to enrich our understanding by pursuing at least a little the ideas this definition suggests.

Who is this God with whom the holy person is in union? In what is perhaps the most often-quoted citation from Scripture, St. John says that "God is Love" (1 John 4:8 and 16). And so the union with God that constitutes personal holiness is a union with love. It is the presence of love at the center of one's personhood and the power of love as the energy of one's life. Love, that total and self-forgetful commitment in concern, is the axis around which the entire life of personal holiness revolves. Indeed, it is so central to the Christian life that St. John can declare not only that God is Love, but also that Love is God, that "no man has ever seen God; if we love one another, God abides in us" (1 John 4:12).

But where does that love come from? How are we to achieve it? John speaks to this question as well, and his answer is critical to our reflections on personal holiness. "In this is love, not that we loved God but that he loved us. . . . We love, because he first loved us" (1 John 4:10, 19). The love that constitutes personal holiness, then, is something that comes with God's own free presence in our lives, his self-donation. That love is not an achievement of our own. Rather it is a gift of the highest order.

This idea of love as a gift is, of course, in line with our own experience. Love that is not free is not really love at all. The whole thrill of love, the whole wonder of it, lies in this unexpected, unrequired quality. That is why people who are loved describe themselves as "lucky." There is nothing they could have done to guarantee the love they receive. They could only wait and hope.

But the point of these verses from St. John is that the love which is God, the love which is shared with man in personal holiness, possesses this gratuitous quality to an ultimate degree. To be trusted by divinity, to be appreciated by the infinite, to be loved by him who is love, nothing could exceed man's rightful expectations more than this. If anything in life is gift, it is the love of God for us men.

But if personal holiness is union with God in love, and if love is ultimately a gift, it follows that the holiness we are considering in these meditations is itself, in the last analysis, a gift. And this is a most important lesson. Contrary to the way we often think and act, the fact is that personal holiness is not something we do, not something we attain, but rather something we receive from the loving hand of God. It is a charism, a gift, for which we can only wait and hope.

Now, all this is not to say that we have absolutely nothing to do with the growth of personal holiness within us. Quite the contrary. Gifts not only need to be given, they also need to be received. And it is a safe assumption that the dearth of holiness in our world is the result of just such a failure to receive. As Christians we are not called to become holy, but we are called to accept holiness in our lives. We are called to be willing and enthusiastic receivers. And that call is for us a true and difficult demand. We must stop standing in the way of personal holiness, we must cease blockading ourselves from its entrance. From the position of being closed to the presence of holiness we must move to a stance of openness and readiness.

In a sense, then, this is not a book about personal holiness at all. It is a book about receptivity to personal holiness. It is a book about what we can and must do to prepare ourselves for personal holiness and to accept it when it comes. It is a book about the preambles to holiness, about the prerequisites for that reality. If personal holiness really is union with God, this book is about our part in that union. And it willingly leaves God's part to him.

These, then, are some of the implications of my definition of personal holiness. Not all of them, of course. But enough for now. For we have a direction, a perspective to guide us in the coming pages. We went looking for that definition, and we have come to see more clearly the task that lies before us. We tried to answer the question, "What are you talking about?" and our answer has generated questions of its own.

But that is as it should be. After all, this is only our starting point, not our conclusion. Definitions may not be avoidable, but they are not exhaustive, either. What is personal holiness? It is the reality of union with God. That is our definition. Now we are ready to begin.

Chapter Two

MYSTERY

The Christian faith is somehow involved with mystery. At certain levels its message is a proclamation of mystery, and at various points it demands that we face mystery. We speak of "mysteries of the faith." We remember those events of history, the passion, death, resurrection and ascension of Jesus, which are collectively termed "the paschal mystery." And we watched the Second Vatican Council spend much of its time seeking to explain "the mystery of the Church." The Christian faith is involved with mystery.

But if this is true, then it is to be expected that in the quest for personal holiness, we too must consider the reality of mystery. We must try to sort out and understand the import of mystery for our lives as human persons and, even more, for our lives as Christians. But that is no simple task. And particularly for those of us who seek to be Christians in twentieth century America, the struggle with mystery presents major difficulties. For, if the truth be told, our society has a prejudice against mystery.

Where does that prejudice come from? It is hard to say. Perhaps its source is that pragmatism which is so characteristic of American society, that all-consuming commitment to expediency, to "making things work," to looking for results. Or perhaps the source is to be found in the techno-logical emphasis of our culture. In the United States technology is pivotal, technology is ulti-mate, technology is king.

Or at least that used to be the case. For in recent years there appear to be some shifts in the American vision, and we are no longer quite so sanguine about the supremacy of technology. Pragmatists such as John Dewey said that uni-versal education would solve our problems. But it did not. Physical scientists said that the experi-mental method would lead us all to "the good life." But it has not. Businessmen asserted that competitive capitalism would yield a healthy economy and a happy populace. But this promise, too, has not been fulfilled. And so the preem-inence of technology is being questioned. And the notion of mystery is being reexamined.

We should participate in that reexamination. But in doing so, we must be careful not to overstate the case. For mystery is not a name to be given to whatever is still unknown. Mystery is not a shorthand excuse for ignorance. And mystery must not be a rationalization for inaction. Men of earlier ages tended to use the word in this way. They tended to label as mystery any fact which had not yet been grasped, any cause which had not yet been isolated, any phenomenon which had not yet been explained. And it was this conception of mystery which tempted men of our time to reject the idea entirely.

What, then, is the proper understanding of mystery? Perhaps an example will help to answer the question.

All of us have had the experience of "dry knowledge" in our lives. Perhaps it was during the period of our schooling, or perhaps it was in the midst of a dull and uninteresting dinner conversation. But whatever the context, the experience was the same. We were faced with knowledge without appreciation, with facts without enthusiasm. We heard the information, we gathered the data. And when we were done, we were struck by the insignificance of it all. What we had learned seemed to make no difference, and therefore we didn't care.

On the other hand, we have all had the opposite experience as well. We have felt the delight that comes with real stimulation. We have become excited by an idea or an insight or an understanding. Perhaps we started out simply "to know." But we ended up "appreciating" as well. An exciting teacher, a fascinating dinner partner, an awe-inspiring spouse—many sorts of people can be the occasion of this experience. But whatever its source, we consider ourselves gifted, indeed, when we are its recipients.

And that experience is what we mean by mystery. Mystery is not the realm of the not-yet-known. It is the realm of the intrinsically unknowable. Or perhaps more precisely, mystery is the realm of those realities which are not known in that technological, objective, scientific way that our society has usually emphasized. Mysteries are known in another way. They are known through a sort of intuition, through a perception, through a deep and profound and genuine appreciation. The realm of mystery is the realm of the aesthetic, the artistic. It is the realm of beauty. The realm of mystery is the realm of values, of appreciation (*ad pretium*, toward value). And consequently it is the realm of wonder.

Let us go deeper. The difference between ordinary knowledge and the knowledge of mystery can be seen in our stance as knowers. Ordinary knowledge is the servant of us men, and we are its masters. We stand over that knowledge, we take it up, we make it our own, and we put it to use. In our colloquial language we speak of "mastering the facts," of comprehending and apprehending the truth. And all of these words and expressions convey a similar image: the image of taking in, of grasping, of controlling and of using. But when we speak of the sort of evaluative knowledge that we have of mystery, our language is quite otherwise. We go out of ourselves and understand these sorts of truths. We experience a sort of ecstasy, a standing outside of ourselves. We dare not try to "grasp" mystery; at most we can gently "embrace" it. In the final analysis, we do not pull mystery to ourselves as our servant. Rather we go out of ourselves and serve that mystery which is larger than ourselves.

So the notion of mystery refers to a different sort of knowing in the human person. It refers to a sort of evaluative, insightful perception rather than merely to a factual comprehension. The notion of mystery refers, also, to a different sort of reality which that richer knowing reveals to us.

We might say that ordinary knowing reveals the truth to us as two-dimensional. It describes for us the length and width of reality, and it does so with considerable accuracy. The picture given us by ordinary knowledge can be duplicated. One can trace that picture, so to speak, and make additional copies of it in the mind of another. The knowledge of mystery, on the other hand, reveals to us the third dimension of reality. It opens to our understanding the depth, the richness, the density of reality. And for that very reason it is not nearly so susceptible to communication. The knowledge of mystery, unlike ordinary knowledge, is an intensely personal and individual experience. But for that very reason it is the most precious knowledge of all.

So much for our stumbling attempt to describe the idea of mystery. Now, as persons seeking holiness within the Christian faith, we must ask a further question. Very simply, what is it that is mystery for the Christian? And here we find many answers.

Certainly God himself is the first and foremost mystery of our Christian experience. Not so much the fact of God, his mere existence. Philosophers, too, can come to that piece of knowledge. Rather the question of who God is remains a mystery for the Christian. What sort of person, or persons, is the God whom we worship? What is he up to in this world? Why, in the last analysis, does he act as he does in our regard? These are questions which have faced and perplexed Christians in every age. And they are questions which always will do so. For these questions point towards the mystery in our lives.

And if God is a mystery for us, certainly the Son of God, Jesus Christ, is a mystery as well. Again, not the mere fact of Jesus Christ. Any historian can tell us that such a man existed once upon a time, that he worked some sorts of wonders, that he preached and proclaimed a message, and that he died. Even the abstract idea that such a man was God can be discussed with ordinary knowledge. But the richer, three-dimensional reality of Christ can only be appreciated in mystery. The power of love in this person, the claim he makes upon us, the good news that he authoritatively announces, all of these realities go beyond the realm of fact and enter the realm of mystery. And as such they demand that we stand before them as servants. The facts about Jesus Christ are something we question. But the mystery of Jesus Christ is something that questions us.

But the mysteries of the Christian life are not limited even to the persons of the Trinity. Indeed for the Christian, and precisely because he is Christian, the whole world is a mystery. There is a pregnancy to our world, a richness and meaning, that the Christian must not overlook. When we say that the world is created by God, we are not merely enunciating a description of omnipotent power. We are not merely conceding the fact that some divine energy is responsible for this reality. Rather we are addressing the astonishing truth of the fertile love of God, exploding out of himself into the empty beyond.

If it is somewhat true that, as the fact-knowers

say, the world is a well-oiled machine, it is not altogether true. Why do we live in a world that is technicolor and not merely monochrome? Why are there thousands of species of birds, and not merely the half dozen species required by different climates? Why, indeed, is creation so fantastically, incomprehensibly huge? No, beyond all the facts of our world there stands the mystery of our world. And it is a mystery that calls not for haughty comprehension but for humble appreciation. Whatever else may be said about God, he may not be described as "thrifty" in his use of creative power. The world which we appreciate in its mystery reveals a God of lavishness, of extravagance, indeed, of utter prodigality. And in the face of that divine effusiveness, one can only stand in wonder.

Thus, we see the mystery of God and the mystery of God's world. But we see more. We see the mystery of ourselves. Indeed, perhaps the greatest of all mysteries, or at least the most astonishing, is the mystery of me. Who am I? Why am I? What am I up to, and where am I going? All these are questions to which the factual answers seem utterly inadequate.

Have you ever listened to someone describing you, attempting to capture the essence of your personality? How frustrating such an experience is, how irritating. The fact of the matter is that no person, no matter how sensitive, no matter how close, can fully grasp the meaning of me. And so I interrupt his description, I take over the task he has begun. I verbalize for myself the qualities and attributes and attitudes which constitute my personhood. And as I do so I confront the most frustrating reality of all. I fail, as well! Not only are others incapable of capturing my essence, I am incapable of doing so. Not only am I a mystery to those with whom I live in this world, I am a mystery to myself.

Other men miss the subtleties of my personality because of a certain opaqueness that I have. They cannot penetrate the murky depths of my soul in order to see and grasp my core. It is simply too far for them to go. But by the same token, I miss the intricacy and complexity of myself because I am too close. It is an intriguing fact that of all the physical things in this world, there is only one that I cannot see. Myself. I can see my mirror image, I can see photographic reproductions of myself. But I can never see the original, live reality of me. Similarly, the eye of my mind is ultimately incapable of seeing the inner reality that I am. No matter how deeply into my heart and mind and soul I seek to penetrate, no matter how deeply I succeed in penetrating, I never touch the utter center of myself. For that center is always the subject that is looking. And consequently it can never be the object that is seen.

So that is the first sense in which I am a mystery

to myself: the central reality of my personhood is beyond the ambit of my perception. But I am also a mystery in another, deeper sense. Namely, I am not the sort of reality that is *meant* to be known by ordinary knowledge.

I am not merely present in this or that place, I do not merely exist as a fact. Much more importantly I am alive. There is a wellspring of vitality and energy within me which is ultimately inexplicable. No matter how much study and investigation I do, no matter whether I seek the aid of a psychoanalyst or undergo some form of therapy, I never succeed in forming a definitive answer to the question that I am. And what is more, this power within me is something which I experience not as my servant, but as my master. In some strange paradoxical sense, I am the servant of my own self, I stand accountable to that self. I find myself laden with an obligation to be what I am, to construct the facticities of my life in accord with the deeper power of my person.

So there I am. I cannot know myself. I cannot rule myself. Ultimately I can only stand in wonder at myself. For ultimately I am a mystery to me.

That is what we mean by mystery in the Christian life. It is a different sort of knowing pointed towards a different sort of reality. It encompasses God and the world and myself. But what does this have to say about the search for Christian holi-

ness? It seems to me it has much to say. And perhaps we should briefly isolate at least a few points
here.

It is sometimes argued that Christians are
different from other men in that they know more,
that they are more in touch with the meaning of
the world. And I believe that statement is true,
but only if properly understood. To say that
Christians stand out as knowing more than other
men is not to arrogantly and condescendingly
claim some special collection of facts. It is not to
assert that we Christians are the privileged posses-
sors of objective truths which others do not know.
Quite the contrary, it is to assert that we are
possessed in a way that other men are not. Precisely as Christians, we stand explicitly and consciously in the face of mystery. We acknowledge
that mystery, we affirm it, and we seek to appreciate it. We accept its hold upon us, the response
and the allegiance which it demands. And so if we
Christians understand reality better than do other
men, it is only because we stand under that reality
to a fuller and deeper extent.

This vision of Christian knowing points, in
turn, to a second point. Our identity as Christians
does not utterly remove us from the society in
which we live. And consequently we are tempted
like all men to infatuation with technical knowledge. Even in the inner reality of our spiritual life,

we can be sorely tempted to reduce mystery to the level of mere knowing. We can look too quickly in Scripture for specific and "useful" answers. We can expect the Church or the Sacraments or the teachings of our faith to speak to us with a scientific clarity. And if we do so, the effects will be tragic indeed. To give in to the technological temptation does not merely inhibit the Christian faith, it utterly eviscerates it.

Our reflections on the idea of mystery contribute, thirdly, to a deeper understanding of the role of prayer in the development of personal holiness. Prayer, of course, is many things. And in another meditation we shall consider more fully what they are. But the central place of mystery in the Christian faith should make it clear that if it is anything, prayer is an exercise in wonder. If in prayer we speak the words "Lord hear us," all the more must we speak the words, "Thanks be to God." If we ask for illumination in our worship of God, all the more must we celebrate the darkness. To put all this another way: perhaps we would do a better job of describing the prayer of the Christian person if we compared it, not to any intellectual exercise such as study or reflection, but rather to the exercise of the human aesthetic sense. Prayer is like listening to a beautiful piece of music, to viewing a wonderful painting or a breathtaking sunset. Prayer is not learning, it is celebration. And all this because the object and the subject of prayer, God and man, are mysteries.

This personal holiness, finally, which we are considering in this book, is itself a mystery. For it is the gift of a mysterious God that transforms a mysterious human person. The path to holiness which we desire to walk is a mysterious path, not clear, not objective, not utterly explainable, and certainly not measurable. It is a uniquely personal path, a road we each walk for the first and only time. And thus if the words we share about personal holiness are stumbling words, if we end up not so much instructing one another as inviting one another's appreciation, we ought not to be surprised.

It seems that our culture is regaining a consciousness of mystery. If that is so, it is good. For such a consciousness has always been and must always be at the core of the Christian faith.

Chapter Three

THE NEARBY/FARAWAY GOD

When all is said and done, the search for personal holiness is nothing more or less than a search for God. And in comparison with this goal all the other benefits of holiness are of minimal importance. The development of a greater degree of personal integration, that feeling of inner peace and joy with oneself, a sense of order and purpose in one's life, all of these realities are certainly desirable. But none of them are of any ultimate value unless they are achieved and maintained in the context of an abiding sense of the loving presence of God.

Consequently, as we consider all the various facets of the topic of personal holiness, no topic demands our attention so forcefully as does the question of God. Where is God to be found? In what ways is he part of my life? How can I perceive his presence, and how shall I understand it?

These are, perhaps, the ultimate questions. And they are the questions which concern us in this meditation.

One of the major themes of our Judeo-Christian heritage has been that of the presence of God. It is something on which our convictions are deep and long-lasting. At the very beginning of the history of our salvation Yahweh says to Abraham: "I will establish my covenant between me and you and your descendants after you throughout their generations for an everlasting covenant, to be God to you and to your descendants after you" (Gen. 17:7). When the prophets begin to speak of a "new covenant," they keep the same perspective: "I will make a new covenant. . . . I will put my law within them, and I will write it upon their hearts; and I will be their God, and they shall be my people" (Jer. 31:31, 33). When this new covenant comes to be in Jesus Christ, the meaning of that Christ is captured in the name *Emmanuel*, which means "God with us." And finally, near the close of Scripture, in the Book of Revelation, the following words appear: "I heard a great voice from the throne saying, 'Behold, the dwelling of God is with men. He will dwell with them, and they shall be his people, and God himself will be with them' " (Rev. 21:3).

But these words, and the convictions which underlie them, do not altogether answer our question. For in my life, at least, the presence of God is far more a goal to be hoped for than it is a reality to be enjoyed. God is obscure in my life, and the search for him continues. So the question remains, where and how is God to be found?

Some people say that God is to be found primarily in the message of the Church and in the preaching of her ministers. They consider that God is not immediately present to any of us in an experiential way, but rather that he must be passed on to us in the line of tradition that goes back to the Apostles. It was the first members of the Church who immediately and sensibly experienced God in their lives. And Christ, in establishing the Church, authorized them to pass on the message grounded in their own experience. The seven sacraments, of course, provide a certain sort of direct experience of God. But this experience utterly depends on the faith with which they are received. And that faith in turn comes from the message which has been proclaimed. Thus I find God in the sacraments because and to the extent that I have been told to find him there. For people of this persuasion, then, the search for God is primarily an exercise in docility, a willingness to be taught the truths which reveal him to us.

This approach to the presence of God, to be sure, has much to commend it. For one thing, it is an approach which has a basis in the scriptural word of God. As St. Paul says: "How are men to call upon him in whom they have not believed? And how are they to believe in him of whom they have never heard? And how are they to hear without a preacher? And how can men preach unless they are sent? . . . So faith comes from what is heard, and what is heard comes by the preaching of Christ" (Rom. 11:14, 17).

And for another thing, this understanding has a certain reasonableness. When God created this world, so the argument goes, he created it with its own purposes and its own laws of existence. And the value of creation comes precisely from conformity to those laws of being, the natural laws. For God to capriciously intrude upon his creation, however, would violate those laws at least in the sense of superseding them. Consequently God does so as little as possible.

The mystery of our salvation, of course, required the entrance of the Son of God into this world so that his divine power could gift us with union with God. But within the general understanding of those who hold this view, the wonder of the Incarnation lies precisely in the fact that it is the utterly singular example of the direct presence of God in his creation. Apart from the reality of the Incarnation, the world of nature is left to follow its own laws, to be what it is and nothing more. And it is for this reason, then, that preaching and proclamation must continue. For they represent the only way by which the wonder of that Incarnation can be communicated to succeeding generations of men.

But there is another way of understanding the presence of God in his world, a way which is equally rooted in the traditions of Scripture. And that way holds that nothing in our experience is simply what it seems, but rather that everything is more than it seems. The finite world may seem to be just a created reality following its own laws, but in fact it is the sacrament of the presence of God. God does not stand over against or apart from his creation nearly as much as he stands within and behind it. And consequently every sensible reality with which we are in contact contains within itself another reality, is pregnant with the presence of God. In this understanding, then, preaching does not function as the announcement of a God who in fact lives far away, but rather as the explanation by which men are invited to open their eyes and to see the God who is very near indeed.

I mentioned that this understanding of the presence of God is rooted also in Scripture. Consider, for example, the very beginning of the Gospel of John: "In the beginning was the Word, and the Word was with God, and the Word was God. He was in the beginning with God; all things were made through Him, and without Him was not anything made that was made" (John 1:1–3).

Or again, listen to the words of St. Paul: "He is the image of the Invisible God, the first-born of all creation; for in Him all things were created, in heaven and on earth. . . . He is before all things, and in Him all things hold together" (Col. 1:15–17).

In these scriptural citations, and in many others with a similar message, the point is that the Word of God is the model for all that God has created. When this world came into being, it was not given just any shape at all. Rather it was patterned on the second Person of the Trinity, it was made to conform to him. Thus, when the Word entered history in Jesus Christ, what occurred was not the intrusion of a stranger into a new land, but rather a sort of divine homecoming. Again, as St. John said, when Jesus came into this world "he came to his own home" (John 1:11). He joined his own reflections, as it were. The Image of God met the images of himself, and brought them to fulfillment. And thus the entrance of the Son of God into history in Jesus Christ did not constitute the beginning of God's presence in the world, but rather its climax.

But what does all this have to do with our personal holiness? It was for the sake of our spiritual lives that we pursued these thoughts, and now we must see what difference they make.

The point of these reflections is that the presence of God is a very real part of our world, and of our experience, if only we will see. The beauty of nature, the wonders of technology and culture, the power of human relationships, all of these are capable of speaking to us of God if only we will let them. And if God is absent from us, it is not because he stands apart from this world. Rather it is only because our capacity and willingness to experience him are so sadly limited.

We are really far more blessed than we think. In the last analysis we do not need any person or any institution to introduce God and his presence into our lives. He is, on the contrary, immediately present to us all. Or more precisely, he is present through the mediation of the One Mediator, Jesus Christ our Lord. And apart from him we need no other.

This is not to say that we do not require the ministry of the Church in our spiritual journey to God. It is only to specify that ministry. The Church does not so much make God present to the Christian person as it does reveal the presence which is already there. In Jesus Christ God is part of our world if we will only see. And we need the Church to help us see.

Thus the answer to our question, where is God to be found, is very simple. God is to be found everywhere. But perhaps some further details will help to make this answer clear. For example, does it follow from this answer that all the elements of our experience are equally capable of revealing God? Or does God, so to speak, lie closer to the surface of some experiences than of others? The answer, it seems to me, is the second.

Consider, for instance, the seven sacraments of the Church. Throughout our tradition these liturgical mysteries have played a uniquely important role in the Christian life. Why is that? The reason is that in some way or other they were instituted by Jesus Christ. And this institution rendered the seven sacraments, above all the other sacramental moments of our experience, uniquely transparent with the presence of God. The promise of Jesus is precisely that here, in these experiences, God will more than ever make himself known. And here, in these experiences, the universal mediation of the Word of God will more than ever bear fruit for our lives.

But even apart from the seven sacraments, it seems to me that there is some hierarchy to the sacramentality of creation. The beauty of a sunset and the wonder of a well-wrought piece of music surely do hold the presence of God within them. But if the common testimony of men holds any validity, experiences such as these are far outstripped by the power of human relationships to communicate God. It is preeminently in the relationship of love between human persons that the love of God is mediated and made present within the human community. And perhaps among all human relationships, this is most especially true of the relationship of marriage. When faithful and total love is shared between a husband and a wife, the resulting union fully deserves to be called a sacrament of God's presence, in all the senses of that word. And perhaps at some deeply religious level, this is the very reason why the vast majority of men and women choose to spend their lives in the married state. It is only in marriage, they believe, that they will find personal human fulfillment. And it is preeminently in marriage that they will find God. And these two "finds" are ultimately the same.

But the Church has for many centuries also made a place for those who choose to follow the celibate life-style. Indeed, it has held such people in high esteem. What shall we say of celibates? Are they persons who opt to encounter God in some more direct and non-sacramental way? Are they persons who critique our whole understanding of the presence of God by choosing a quite different alternative? By no means. Rather the value of the celibate life-style lies precisely in its affirmation of the universality of the sacramental presence of God. The celibate reminds us that God is to be found not only in the loving presence of a single other person, but also in absolutely every moment of our lives.

Whether one chooses to be married or to be

celibate, of course, is ultimately a matter of individual gift. Every man must attempt to become what he senses himself to be called to be. And thus for the individual person, only one alternative may be viable. Still, perhaps it will help our understanding of the presence of God to visualize the way in which these two styles of life complement each other. Consider the following example.

The presence of God in his world, it seems to me, is like the light of the sun which shines upon our lives. That light is everywhere, and even on the darkest, most cloud-covered day it makes its presence felt. But it is particularly appreciated on bright and clear days when its shining magic can work upon us directly and with strength. And when the rays of the sun are focused with a magnifying glass, as children delight in doing, then is its power made consummately apparent.

The relationship of marriage is like that magnifying glass. With its help the light of God's presence is brightened and strengthened and made supremely intense. Under the magnifying glass of marriage the human person is more able to experience the presence of God than he is anywhere else. And for the person whose eyes are suited to that intensity, there is quite literally no other place to be.

But not everyone's eyes are so suited. Within the Church there always have been and always will be certain individuals whose eyes are more comfortable in the dusk and dawn of God's light. They have, as it were, a sort of night-vision which permits them to detect the glimmers of God across the whole surface of the world. Even this night-vision, of course, does not make it easy to pick out the details of the landscape. Indeed, the peculiar challenge of celibacy is that the one who walks this road must look carefully or he will see nothing at all. But there is no alternative. For just as the one suited to the brightness of marriage would surely stumble in those dark places, so the celibate would be burned by marriage and not warmed.

Still, when these two vocations are well-lived, they complement each other in a most worthwhile way. On the cloudy days of life, when no one can see very well, marriage testifies to the continuing presence of God. It reinforces our weakening faith and rejuvenates our fragile wills. And celibacy, for its part, reminds us not to be so intrigued by the magnifying glass that we forget the light which passes through. It bears witness to that light of God, it proves by its survival that this light is to be found throughout our world. And it reassuringly reports that this light is sufficient for human happiness.

But no matter what the vocation to which each one of us is particularly called, the strategy for the Christian life remains the same. We are called to union with God, we are called to find God. And we find God not by turning away from our world and from our senses, but rather by turning toward our world and using our senses well. If only we will look and listen and understand, God is to be found within the mystery of our experience. For that reason, then, the dynamic of the Christian life, of the life of personal holiness, is not so much one of inviting God in as it is of allowing ourselves to see the God who is there.

To say that this is easy would be foolish indeed. For as I have suggested, the presence of God is not to be found at the very surface of our experience, but rather within its depths. If the world in which we live, if the people with whom we relate, if our own selves are sacraments of the presence of God, they are not on that account transparent with his presence. As a matter of fact, it is the very definition of a sacrament to both reveal and disguise the deeper reality within it. And thus the experience of the presence of God will always be a struggle for us Christians. We will always be tempted to see only what is before our noses, and to miss the more subtle meanings of reality. The world truly is more than it seems, but to our finite eyes it remains opaque, all the same.

And thus when all is said and done we are left with a challenge that cannot be avoided and a paradox that cannot be erased. On the one hand, we believe that our God is very close to us. And at certain peak moments of our lives we can practically taste and touch his loving care in our regard. But at many other moments of our lives, he is not at all close. We search for his presence and his concern in vain, and he seems frighteningly distant from all our needs.

But the Christian faith has always reveled in paradoxes: God, three and one; Jesus, God and man; the lion and the lamb; cross and crown; death and resurrection. So we ought not to be surprised that our search for the presence of God itself leaves us with paradox. Indeed, perhaps we ought to glory in that fact.

Where is God to be found? That was our first question. And the answer was: everywhere. A final question now suggests itself. What God is found when we look? And the painful, paradoxical answer comes back. Our nearby/faraway God.

Chapter Four

PRAYER

Perhaps there is no element of the Christian life so completely identified with the quest for personal holiness as is prayer. And this is as it should be.

In the past, I suppose, the mistake was made of totally identifying prayer and personal holiness. The conviction was held, or at least the impression was given, that the only Christians capable of genuine holiness were those who spent much or all of their time in the practice of prayer. Ordinary people, people who found it necessary to spend the vast majority of their time in the tasks of living, were relegated to some secondary status in the Christian community. And this is a misunderstanding which we must definitely seek to eliminate. All Christians are called to holiness, and all Christians are capable of holiness.

But if prayer is not everything in the Christian

life, still it is something. Indeed, it is an extremely important element in the development of our faith. So our attempt to reflect on the meaning of personal holiness in our lives surely demands that we consider at length the reality of prayer.

What precisely is prayer? Needless to say, it is, in the last analysis, a deep and impenetrable mystery. And so no definition will express its reality with complete adequacy. But men have always tried to define it, or at least describe it. And so must we.

Prayer is the raising of the mind and heart to God. That is one definition that has often been given. Or prayer is man's act of communicating himself to God. Or perhaps more profoundly, prayer is the arena within which God and man communicate themselves to each other. These are all good definitions, capturing important aspects of the mystery of prayer. But I believe I would say simply that prayer is the conscious and human union of God and man.

The last words of this definition of mine are, of course, repeated from my initial definition of personal holiness. Only the two modifiers make it different. But to me they make a very important difference, as I now hope to show.

I say that prayer is a conscious union. What does this mean? There have been suggestions at times in the history of the Church that everything we do is prayer. And there certainly is a sense in which this is true. Nonetheless it seems to me that to define prayer in such a broad fashion makes the term virtually meaningless. To say that prayer is everything in general is, in some paradoxical way, to say that it is nothing in particular. So while there is no denying that the Christian in the state of grace stands in constant union with his God, I would limit the term prayer to those moments when he is conscious of that union.

And prayer is a human union. This term deserves some explanation. I am not saying merely that prayer is *of necessity* human. I am not merely focusing on the fact that man is the one who prays and that therefore no prayer is possible outside of the human style. The fact that prayer is human is not some unfortunate but unavoidable limitation. Rather it is the glory of prayer. For if the Incarnation of Jesus Christ means anything, it means that God effects salvation, brings his gift of life and spirit, and shares himself with man on human terms and not on his own. Indeed, this mystery of the Incarnation, as it reveals God's intention, is the great wonder of the Christian faith.

Throughout the history of man, religions have emerged as an attempt to explain the world of man and the destiny of man. And a common theme in these religions has always been the theme of salvation. Man experiences the need to be saved, and man believes in a God who will save him. But in most cases the religions which have developed in the human community have conceived of this salvation in terms of escape from the world. Man becomes one with God, so their beliefs go, by turning his back on the world in which he lives, by forsaking his human desires and human wishes, and by retreating into the realm of the divine. God calls man to himself, away from the world of man and into his own world.

The Christian faith, however, is quite otherwise. The good news of Jesus Christ is precisely that the gift of salvation which man seeks is to be found in his very midst. God dwells with man and not vice versa, and the love of God is expressed through love of neighbor.

So to declare that prayer is a human union between God and man is not to make a concession but rather to proclaim a boast. It is also, and not incidentally, to specify the strategy for these reflections. For if prayer is a reality of human union, then it should exhibit many of the characteristics of human union. And we should be able to learn the dynamic of prayer by looking at ourselves and by considering the dynamic of the human unions which we seek and experience.

Consequently, I would like to suggest here eleven qualities of prayer. And while it would be a bit of an exaggeration to say that these qualities are simply being applied to prayer after having been found in our ordinary human experience, still we will not be surprised to discover that they are very ordinary, very common, very human qualities indeed. They are the fruit, as it were, of the marriage between faith and human experience.

The first quality of prayer, then, is gratitude. Gratitude, of course, has always been at the heart of the Christian faith. The central act of the Mass is known as the Eucharistic Prayer, the prayer of gratitude. And the very last words of the liturgy are "thanks be to God." But gratitude is also an extremely important component of human union.

I recall as a child being asked by my father why I had not spoken to a man who had given me a gift. I responded that I was too embarrassed, too shy to speak to him. I remember very clearly my father's reply: "The one thing you must never hesitate to say is thank you. Everyone has a need to hear those words. And so you can be quite sure that when you speak them they will be well received."

Gratitude is always appreciated and always cherished by those who receive it. And so in our union with God, gratitude should be a principal focus.

Secondly, prayer ought, it seems to me, to involve a genuine willingness to ask, to reveal oneself as needy. We human beings work so hard to be strong, to be competent, to be self-sufficient, that we find it extremely difficult to ask for help. Somehow the request for assistance seems to imply some inadequacy, some failure on our part. And this we hate to concede.

But that hesitancy is really very sad. For when a person commits himself in relationship he does not only want to be appreciated and cared for, he also wants to be needed. The need to be needed, indeed, is one of the deepest urges in us. And consequently, in human exchange we do one another a real service when we openly admit our needs and express those needs through requests for help.

In a similar way, it seems to me that I do God a service, and pay him a compliment, when I willingly and forthrightly admit my need for his presence and aid in my life. The simple fact is that I cannot live without him. And that fact is something I ought to openly affirm.

Thirdly, prayer ought to be marked by a simple sharing with God. Not by many words, not even by a constant and intense attention, but by simple sharing. How many human relationships have been injured or even destroyed by too narrow a focus and too exclusive a concern for the other party. We look with wry amusement at the adolescent couple who have lost sight of the whole world in the bright glow of each other's personalities. We know that such an all-consuming relationship cannot survive. Not only can their individual personalities not withstand such constant and intense scrutiny, but also the relationship itself demands the nourishment of other experiences and other people to keep it healthy.

This is an insight which has been ratified from many directions. I think, for example, of the old cliché, "familiarity breeds contempt." If the cliché is not always true, still it can often be true. I think too, of the testimony of a number of young married couples. They report that the arrival of their first child was extremely important in the development of their own marital relationship. For it got their attention off of themselves and on to a common task in which they both shared. "It is the building of a family," they say, "which nourishes in a genuine way the relationship between ourselves."

Even the anatomy of the human being hints at this same idea. Have you ever noticed how when an injured football player is helped from the field, he is supported by men who stand at his side? Whether it is a coincidence or not, the fact is that the human body is best helped when the support stands, not eye-to-eye with the needy person, but shoulder-to-shoulder with him looking out in the same direction. And similarly, our union with God is nourished not only by the times when we direct our attention exclusively to him, but also by the times when we simply and honestly share with him the tasks in which we are involved.

This quality of prayer is, I believe, of particular significance to ordinary Catholics. For, as I suggested at the beginning of this meditation, members of the Church have often been tempted in the past to infer that only those with the leisure for extensive "total prayer" are capable of personal holiness. And this quality suggests that that is not true. Any Christian is capable of nourishing his union with God through prayer, no matter what his circumstance or situation. All that is required is the occasional consciousness of the presence and concern of God and a willingness to share with him the activities of one's life. This any person can do, and this every Christian should do.

Fourthly, prayer ought to involve sharing with other people. How easily we forget the social nature of man when we turn to the topic of prayer. And how easily we overlook the need for sharing in this rich and important aspect of the Christian life. But it must not be overlooked. Just as every healthy relationship is in some sense non-exclusive, so it is with the relationship of prayer. A strong life of prayer inevitably demands that the experience be shared with those around us. And, in a paradoxical way, the life of prayer is itself strengthened in the very act of sharing.

What is more, inasmuch as all Christians together comprise the single mystical Body of Christ, the people of God, the life of prayer and personal holiness is a reality pursued in common fully as much as it is individually. In the last analysis it is not your prayer life and my prayer life, it is our common and shared life of prayer. Either we nourish and support and challenge one another in our attempts to achieve conscious union with God, or we undermine and inhibit one another's efforts in that direction.

Such sharing of prayer, of course, can take many forms. It may be the official and intrinsically social prayer of the Church. Or it may be the completely informal and spontaneous praying of a small group of friends. But no matter what its form, the spirit of sharing is an essential quality of the prayer life of Christians.

Fifthly, prayer must involve discipline. Perhaps in our time we are less open to the quality of discipline either in prayer or any other aspect of our lives. But it seems obvious to me that this quality must be present.

Sentimental movies and cheap paperback books may suggest that the relationship of love is an utterly spontaneous and free-floating thing. But our experience teaches us that relationships must be carefully and consciously nurtured or they soon die. The care and tending of interpersonal unions is not something that can be left to chance. It must be planned or it will not happen. "We'll have to get together sometime." How often we hear or say those words. But we know full well that unless a specific date is set, unless a concrete commitment is made, and unless the discipline of planning and follow-through is accepted, the encounter will never take place.

In prayer, too, some planning and discipline are essential. In a sense, we human beings have to make an appointment to see God. And this not because of God's limited availability, but rather because of our seemingly infinite capacity to forget.

A sixth quality of prayer is wastefulness. I do not mean a selfish sort of wastefulness, an unconcern about people or things. Rather I am focusing on that sort of wastefulness which exhibits itself in a willingness to "waste time," to share time and attention with another person, no strings attached and no expectations present. And I include this quality to rectify what strikes me as an over-emphasis today.

Our culture highly values the quality of authenticity in human life. It lays great stress on the need to be genuine and sincere in whatever one does. It rebels against an apparent legalism and mechanism which seemed to characterize the era before our own. And it says that the ultimately important thing is not what one does, but why one does it.

This emphasis is laudable, indeed. As a matter of fact, in another place in this book I will adopt this emphasis and warn against the temptation in the Christian life to lose a good intention while keeping good behavior. But at the same time I see a danger for myself and for others in too exclusive a commitment to this idea. There have been times when I considered spending some moments in prayer, but decided not to because I was too tired or too distracted to pray with real fervor. I have had people explain to me that they did not attend Mass because they could not find within themselves a profound and powerful Christian motivation for going. They feared that their attendance would be mere legalism and empty. And what I want to suggest to myself and to others is that empty actions can be worthwhile.

We do not expect our every encounter with our fellow man to be rich in significance and overwhelmingly memorable. Husbands and wives do not expect the total and passionate attention of their spouse at every moment, nor are they capable of giving that attention. But such people do not for that reason stay completely apart, either. They intuitively know that even a minimal sharing, the willingness to simply be together, serves a purpose in the nourishment of their relationship. And they also know that if they waited for that "electric moment" before they spoke to one another, the silence might be literally deadening.

So it is with prayer as an element in the search for personal holiness. Authenticity is most certainly a critical value in the Christian life. But an overweening concern for authenticity must not be allowed to stand in the way of simple ordinary sharing between God and man. We must invite God into our lives not only because at certain moments we feel an overwhelming desire to do so, but also because as a perduring theme of our lives we know that we ought to do so. And to the extent that we are willing to waste time with God, the electric moments of thorough authenticity will, I believe, come of their own free accord.

The seventh quality of prayer is connected to what has just been said. And that is the quality of patience. There is nothing, in my experience, that can so thoroughly destroy a pleasant evening out with friends as "great expectations." Large hopes have a way of destroying small pleasures, and excessive planning almost always leads to disappointment. And so in the pursuit of a life of prayer it is extremely important to avoid those expectations and hopes and plans.

We pray in order to stand in a conscious union with our God. And just as human relationships require great periods of time before they achieve the full union which is their goal, so we must expect the life of prayer to be organic and slow-moving in its development toward the union which is its goal. In the life of the world, "pushy people" are rarely appreciated. In the life of prayer, they must be somewhat offensive to God as well.

Generosity is the eighth quality of prayer, and an extremely important quality it is. For it reminds us of the deeply theological nature of our prayer life. There is a temptation in prayer, as in every relationship, to become manipulative and self-seeking in one's actions. There is a temptation in prayer, as in other relationships, to think of what one can get rather than of what one can give. And this quality spotlights and attacks that temptation. It reminds us that we Christians love God because he has loved us first. And through prayer we seek a conscious union with him because he has already sought a conscious union with us. Thus, prayer really is a self-gift of the Christian to his God, a gift which ought to be made as generously and altruistically as possible.

I recall the advice given by a preacher some years ago regarding the frequent reception of Communion. He pointed out that many people tend to limit their reception of Holy Communion because of their own sense of unworthiness. They do not feel they deserve the regular recurring presence of the Lord to them, and so they stay away. The preacher's point was that such an understanding totally misconstrues the sacrament of the Eucharist. It should be clear from the fact that Jesus instituted this sacrament that it is his genuine and sincere desire to be one with us in its reception. And if this is the case, who are we to refuse him that request? Is, then, the decision to stay away from the sacrament an expression not of humility, but rather of pride? And ought we not to swallow that pride and let the Lord be with us as he wills?

It seems to me this same point should be made with regard to prayer. The union between man and God is a gift God genuinely wishes to bestow on us. And he asks of us above all the generosity to cooperate in his intention. God desires to bless us, and to fill us with his life and joy. And consequently, when we give ourselves to a spirit of prayer in our lives we are not only participating in the communication of this gift, we are also in some strange way doing God a favor. This favor is what the quality of generosity invites.

Prayer also ought to include the quality of variety. And this precisely inasmuch as prayer is a *human* union with God. As human beings we are subject to all sorts of change in our lives. At one moment we are exuberant, and at another we are depressed. At some times there is a calmness to our lives, and at other times we are filled with agitation. And this fact of variety is something that cannot be escaped. Consequently, our prayer should willingly cooperate in the human need for variety. We ought not to apologize for the fact that at different moments in our lives different forms of prayer seem to meet our needs more fully. There are times when we find it quite easy to speak with the Lord with freedom and facility. At other times, however, we find it necessary to speak in formulas, in the prayers we learned as children. And this should come as no surprise.

What is more, variety is useful in human life not only because of our changing moods, but also because of our tendency toward boredom. Even the most delightful experiences of life become tedious with excessive repetition. And so it is with prayer. Often enough, people will mention that a form of prayer they found useful and rewarding for a long time has suddenly become burdensome to them. No longer can they read the scriptures with appreciation, or pray the rosary, or quietly speak to the Lord in their hearts. They sense the need for some change, but they feel guilty about that change. They feel that moving away from this form will imply some criticism of its validity. And my point is that this need not be the case.

Forms and tools of prayer can be extremely valuable in themselves, and extremely valuable to us at some points in our lives, without being equally valuable at all times. And so we ought not to be hesitant in responding to the felt need for variety in our search for conscious human union with God. For variety is, indeed, an authentic quality of prayer.

In several of the qualities of prayer we have considered so far, the social nature of the Christian life has been emphasized. And this is most appropriate. But it is also important for us to focus on the deeply personal quality of that life. And so as the tenth quality I suggest solitude. Particularly in the lives that so many of us live, with their hectic pace and their numberless superficial relationships, a time of solitude is truly important. Indeed, it is a fundamental human need.

A social commentator suggested some time ago that the current attempt to encourage car-pools for commuting workers is doomed to failure. And the reason why it will fail, he said, is that the car has become much more than a simple mode of transportation. For many people it is the one time in their day when they are alone. And as such, the car has come to serve a deeply important psychological purpose. The time we spend driving from place to place is one of the rare times when we can simply think. We need not feel guilty about the hundred and one tasks we have to do, for being on the road prevents our doing them. And consequently we can at last indulge the human desire to reflect and ruminate about the experiences of our lives.

As this sort of solitude is necessary in our human experience, so it is necessary in our relationship with God. No matter what nourishment we can achieve in common experiences of worship and prayer, these will eventually prove fruitless if they are not complemented by periods of quiet, interior, personal prayer. Whether these moments of solitude occur in a church, or while going for a walk, or hidden in some private room, or, indeed, while driving in the car, is not important. What is important is that they take place. Solitude demands a position in our lives. And it demands a position in our prayer as well.

The final quality of our prayer is flexibility. By this I mean to point out that all I have said about prayer is but the beginning of what needs to be learned. Indeed, all of us spend our whole lives in learning to pray, as we spend them in learning to live. No matter how much we know, no matter how much fulfillment we have experienced, there is much more still in the future. And so as Christians searching for personal holiness in relationship to God, we dare not settle down in any comfortable styles of the past. We must be willing to change, to grow, to learn.

The mystery of our union with God is a mystery which can never be utterly plumbed. And so we must always be prepared to be surprised by some new and startling approach. Perhaps we will discover some other qualities of prayer that are far more important than those listed here. Perhaps we will come upon modes or tools of prayer which are far more useful than those we have previously known. So be it. Flexibility, openness to the future, is the one quality we can never afford to lose.

There are many characteristics which help to define the human personhood of man. But certainly one of those characteristics is the human ability to know. Our consciousness is one of the privileges of human life, and it is one of the tools by which that life can be lived most fully. And consequently the conscious pursuit of union with God is one of the most important characteristics of the Christian life. That conscious union, as I have suggested, is what we mean by prayer.

Prayer is not everything in a Christian life, just as consciousness is not everything in human life. But neither can life do without the conscious element. Every Christian is called to be a man or woman of prayer. And the search for personal holiness will surely depend to a large extent on the degree to which we accept that call.

Chapter Five

ACTION

When St. Benedict first gathered Christian men together in the sixth century to create communities where God might be found and served, he composed a rule of life to aid them in their chosen vocation. And he offered his followers, as a summary of all the details of that rule, a simple three word motto: *Ora et labora*, prayer and work. Benedictine communities across the world still hold that motto today. And well they should. For it has withstood the test of time, and it has proved itself to be a deceptively simple but genuinely profound summary of the Christian life. How does one achieve personal holiness in this world? One achieves it through prayer and action.

And so in our reflections on the topic of personal holiness, it is highly appropriate, indeed essential, that we consider the role of Christian action in our lives.

What do I mean by Christian action? In a sense I mean absolutely everything that we do in the ordinary, day-to-day process of living. But in particular I mean those things that we do with other people, and for their sakes. Action is our way of being present to the world and of making our unique contribution to it. At one moment our action may be focused on the task in which we are commonly engaged. And at another moment it may be focused on the persons with whom we are sharing. But in either case, the function of our action is to involve ourselves in the world and to attempt to make a difference.

There is no doubt that action plays a major part in our Christian lives as a whole. That should be clear from the simple fact of the time we necessarily expend in our activities. But does action play an equally important role in our growth in personal holiness? That is a real question. And all the more so since that role has at times been severely questioned in the past. For example, in his *Imitation of Christ*, St. Thomas à Kempis (surely a holy man) approvingly quotes another author's declaration that "as often as I have been among men, I have returned less a man" (Bk. I, Ch. 20). And he is certainly not unique among teachers of the spiritual life in proposing this "antiaction" view. Notwithstanding these statements, however, it is my deep conviction that Christian action plays a worthy and noble part in our search for personal holiness. And this for a variety of reasons.

First of all, you and I are, when all is said and done, total and indivisible persons. We may divide our lives into parts for purposes of discussion. But in living we must bring those parts together. Each particular component of our lives may have its own unique character. But precisely because of that character, it contributes to the totality of our lives and affects those lives in a specific way. Everything that we do influences everything else that we do, and that influence will in no event be denied. The personal holiness that we are seeking, then, is a holiness of the whole person. And every element of our life either contributes to or stands in the way of that holiness.

What is more, the influence of our activity goes beyond the confines of our own person. It touches the lives of those around us, and it changes them whether we like it or not. The fact that man is a social being means that everyone of us is inevitably involved in the ebb and flow of reciprocal influence. And Christian action is nothing more or less than the way by which we enter that corporate process.

Thus Christian action plays a role in the development of personal holiness because man is a unity and because non-action is, quite literally, impossible. The question is not whether we will participate in Christian action, but rather how that action will take shape. Ignoring the role of Christian action does not eliminate that role, it simply guarantees that the role will be exercised poorly. And, perhaps, in the end destructively.

But if there are human reasons for us to be concerned about Christian action, there are also deeply religious reasons. Indeed, it is one of the boasts of the Christian faith that it has had a great deal to say about the importance of activity. For example, the Gospel of Matthew gives an account of the time when a lawyer asked Jesus a question, to test him. "Teacher, which is the great commandment in the Law?" And he said to him, "You shall love the Lord your God with all your heart and with all your soul and with all your mind. This is the great and first commandment. And a second is like it, you shall love your neighbor as yourself. On these two commandments depend all the Law and the Prophets" (Mt. 22:34–40).

And while Mark and Luke differ in a number of details in their descriptions of this incident, their basic point is exactly the same. Namely, the intimate and irrevocable joining of love of God and love of neighbor in the Christian life. This joining is all the more significant in that while both of these "great commandments" appear elsewhere in scripture (the first in Deut. 6:5; the second in Lev. 19:18), the Old Testament nowhere connects them in the way Jesus does. And so our Christian faith is clear: the love of God and the love of neighbor stand together, or they do not stand at all.

But in what does this love of neighbor consist? Jesus gives us the answer to this question as well: "When the Son of Man comes in his glory, and all the angels with him, then he will sit on his glorious throne. . . . Then the righteous will answer him, 'Lord, when did we see thee hungry and feed thee, or thirsty and give thee drink? And when did we see thee a stranger and welcome thee, or naked and clothe thee? And when did we see thee sick or in prison and visit thee?' And the king will answer them, 'Truly, I say to you, as you did it to one of the least of my brethren, you did it to me' " (Mt. 25:31, 37–40). The love of neighbor is a concrete thing demanding a genuine response to real needs. It is an active thing, a thing of action. Thus, we can say with real justification that the life of Christian holiness is in the last analysis a life of Christian action. Or at least that this action plays an essential and prominent role in that life.

Despite our past tendency to emphasize the negative—the demand that we turn away from what prevents holiness—that we practice self-denial and mortification, it should be clear that the real essence of the Christian life is positive. In the final analysis, we achieve personal holiness not by saying "No" to life, but by saying "Yes." And when we fail ourselves and God through sin, it is much more likely because we have refused to say "Yes" as fully and generously as we ought. We have refused to express our "Yes" through action.

The Church is, of course, the continuation of the life and mission of Jesus in space and time. And therefore in considering the religious reasons for the importance of Christian action, we ought also to take into account the understanding the Church has had of herself and of her task.

Theologians have traditionally said that the Church expresses herself in three characteristic ways. And these are summarized in the three Greek words *liturgia*, *koinonia*, *diakonia* (worship, fellowship, and service). At various times, it is true, one or another of these ways has predominated in the Church's consciousness of herself. But at all times they have each been present. And the full, rich life of the Church demands that all three be strongly represented.

It is not enough, then, for us to express our faith in sincere worship and prayer, nor even for us to join heartily in the common life of the Christian Church. Generous service to our fellow man, authentic Christian action, must also be a hallmark of the follower of Christ. The life of the Church must never be reduced to the level of mere recreation, necessary and rewarding activity which nevertheless stands at the periphery of our lives. No, the Church must be a genuine re-creation, affecting every element of our lives, and expressing itself in all that we do.

The Church is no more real in her moments of worship than she is in moments of social concern. Rather she is real in a different and complementary, but equally essential way. And we who seek to follow Christ are not members of the Church when we passively receive from her the gift of eternal life, but only when we receive *and* share that gift with the world in which we are located.

For all these reasons, then, both human and religious, Christian action plays an utterly critical role in our growth into personal holiness. But to say this is not to provide us with any answers regarding the shape our action ought to take. What really is Christian action? What ought it to look like? And how should it express itself in our lives? These are questions to which there is no definitive answer. But there may be some things which can be said that will help point us toward our own tentative and personal answers. And so, based on the reflections that have been developed thus far in this meditation, I would like to suggest six qualities to Christian action. They are qualities which, it seems to me, ought to be present in every action, no matter what its final shape.

The first quality is engagement. I mean this in

the sense of the French word *engagé*, a genuine connectedness between the self and the situation.

When the Christian involves himself in action in this world, he ought not to operate from some safely removed spiritual platform. He ought not to be like a man standing comfortably on the shore of a swollen river, throwing a rope to those in need, but remaining essentially impassive to their fate. Stoic indifference may well have been an ideal of Greek philosophy, but it is not an ideal in the Christian life. The action to which we are called is an action which involves genuine empathy and sympathy for our brethren in this world. And it demands a willingness to let go of our position of safety, to dive into the murky depths of life, and to risk the possibility of being consumed oneself.

If Jesus Christ, "though he was in the form of God, did not count equality with God a thing to be grasped, but emptied himself, taking the form of a servant," (Phil. 2:6f) we must do the same. We must willingly forsake any pretense of security, and allow our action to express real engagement with our world.

But if, in our Christian action, we ought not to distance ourselves for the sake of our personal safety, there is still a sense in which distance does deserve to be listed among the qualities of that action. For the involvements of the Christian must never absorb him in the world so totally that he loses the capacity to criticize and challenge that world. Precisely because he knows in faith that this world is not all man has, the Christian must always stand a bit apart from the rest of men.

He can be a good and generous citizen of his nation. But when he says "my country right or wrong," he must know full well it can be either. The Christian can dedicate himself to social action, to the improved lot of his fellow man. But he must never pretend that the *genuine* value of this improvement is the *ultimate* value of life.

In other words, we Christians must be willing to live with a tension in our lives of action. We must seek always to be culturally sensitive, to be aware of and in touch with the real needs of our culture, but without becoming utterly acculturated persons ourselves. For if we lose this distance, we not only give up our own most prized possession, a liberating faith in Jesus Christ, but we also sacrifice the very "soul of our apostolate," the attempt to share the experience if not the verbalization of the good news of Jesus Christ.

The third quality of Christian action is practicality. It should be clear from everything I have said thus far that Christian action is not some sort of "spiritual exercise," a sort of religious calisthenic pursued not for its own sake but for the benefit it yields. It is rather the fruit of a genuine concern for the actual needs of those around us.

If the goal of one's physical activity is the development of strong biceps, then it is a matter of some indifference whether one does push-ups or chin-ups. But if the goal is to help a friend who stands on the edge of a cliff, it makes all the difference in the world whether one pushes or pulls. So genuine Christian action must always be oriented toward and proportioned to genuine human need. When the Christian responds in action, he is responding to the call of his situation. And that call must determine the shape his response will take.

We are all familiar with horror stories of sincere Christians, motivated by good will, who nonetheless lumber into complex human situations with consummate insensitivity. They manage to misjudge the needs of the moment, to misunderstand the cultural context, and ultimately to insult the very people they seek to serve. And along the way they make fools of themselves, to say nothing of the gospel. And thus, while it might seem that calling for practical and appropriate Christian action is belaboring the obvious, many sad experiences of our history suggest that it is not.

Fourthly, Christian action ought to have, and quite rightly does have, a particularity about it. To say that every Christian must involve himself in activity in our world is not to say that every Christian must involve himself in exactly the same way. And if our action ought to be a response to the call of the situation, it ought also to be a response to the authentic call of one's own person. The simple fact is that we do not all have precisely the same skills. And thus we cannot all make precisely the same contribution. Indeed, it ought to be the pride of the Christian community that all sorts of skills find expression in the lives of all sorts of people.

We are not all called, for example, to assume the role of radical social critic, adopting the pacifist style of Gandhi, participating in public protests, and perhaps resorting to civil disobedience. But I do not believe that it follows that none of us should assume this role. It is more likely, I think, that our society is blessed by the presence of certain individuals who find within themselves the call to extraordinary and controversial, but ultimately productive, action.

Similarly, in the exercise of my own priestly ministry I prefer to emphasize acceptance and understanding of people, even at the risk of settling for less than the best from those with whom I work. Many of my colleagues, however, adopt precisely the opposite approach. And it seems to me that so long as all of us are motivated by a genuine love for God's people and all of us are for the most part in touch with the genuine needs of those people, the Church ultimately stands to benefit from the diversity of our styles. All of us make a real contribution. And without any of us the Church would be the poorer.

The point, then, is that we ought not to apologize for the diversity of actions pursued by Christians or for the particularity and partialness of each man's contribution. On the contrary, we ought to brag about that. Young people today like to say that every human person ought to "do his own thing." And I would suggest that at least in this sense they are absolutely right.

The fifth quality of Christian action follows from the complexity implied in the last two qualities. Namely, that our action will be, and ought to be, characterized by a certain ambiguity. In the vast majority of cases our Christian faith does not provide us with concrete answers to our human questions. We do not come equipped with an accurate prescription for all that ails our world. The gospel of Jesus demands that each one of us participate in Christian action, but it does not tell us the precise shape this action ought to take. And consequently our efforts to serve our fellow man will of necessity exhibit tentativeness and realistic hesitation.

It is simple honesty to admit that in large part our efforts to walk helpfully into our world involve strides into darkness. We judge that a certain thing is needed. And then we test our judgment in the laboratory of our lives. We hope that our judgment is correct, not only for our own sake but for the sake of those we serve. But if it is not, we stand ready to turn back or change direction. And because of our Christian faith, we live with this ambiguity. We do not use it as an excuse for inaction, but neither do we attempt to ignore it. For the simple truth is that in Christian action we can rarely be sure. And we proceed with our actions in the consciousness of that fact.

Finally, and perhaps most importantly, Christian action must be characterized by universality. If the message of Jesus which we quoted earlier in this meditation means anything at all, it means that our Christian concern must know no limits, must make no exceptions. The parable of the Good Samaritan is prompted by the question put to Jesus: "Who is my neighbor?" And the response given by Jesus is very clear. Does the range of my neighborly concern stop at my family? No, it goes farther. Does it stop at the members of my parish or my city or town? No, farther. Does it stop at the fellow citizens of my nation? At those of my race? No, farther. Who is my neighbor? Everyone!

This is not to say that we Christians are expected to behave toward all our neighbors in precisely the same way. It is clear that parents have a particular sort of responsibility for their children, a sort of responsibility they have for no one else. And no individual person can actively address all the needs of the human community. But the point is that we must *care* about all men and their needs. And that concern must be a deep and genuine part of our lives, whether it is able to bear fruit in concrete action or not. Christian action, no matter what its immediate object, must have the underlying quality of universality. Nothing less will do justice to the universal love we have received from Jesus Christ.

In conclusion, then, Christian life requires Christian action. And this for the very simple reason that life ultimately is action. To stagnate, to be unfruitful, to be permanently silent, to be absolutely still—all these are ways of being dead. And similarly, Christian life that does not issue in action is not life at all, but rather death.

Our attempts to achieve personal holiness must, to be sure, be characterized by a deep and peaceful interiority. We must be willing to be sometimes silent, to pray, to be conscious of the presence and action of God in our lives. But those efforts toward personal holiness must also be characterized by exteriority. By a willingness to go out to our world with care and concern, to involve ourselves and to share the gifts we have received. Interiority and exteriority are partners. They nourish each other, and in the last analysis they depend on each other for their mutual survival.

But if life is ultimately identified with action, action itself must be ultimately identified with love. For in articulating the two great commandments, Jesus did not simply call upon us to "do things" for God and for one another. No, he called upon us to have real and sincere love. He called upon us to bring our fellow men into the embrace of our genuine concern, and on the basis of that concern to act on their behalf. He challenged us to be alive, and to exhibit that sort of life which only a deep love can engender.

It is true that he commanded us to involve ourselves in Christian action. But paradoxically, he commanded us to do so not because we are commanded, but because we care.

The old song suggests that "love makes the world go round." I think the song is right, but I suspect its message is more a condemnation than a commendation. The world, after all, does not go round all that well these days. And if that is true, it can only be because men in general, and we Christians in particular, have never learned to love the way we should.

And therein lies the real force of the call to Christian action.

Chapter Six

CREATORS AND COLLECTORS

It is always dangerous to try to categorize people. To put them in pigeonholes, to separate them into camps, to label them is foolish and ultimately false. We human beings are just too complicated for that. At some point in our life we contradict every category, we deny every principle, we invalidate every label. And we do this for the very simple reason that we contradict ourselves.

What I am suggesting is that man is not properly understood if he is pictured as some sort of jet-stream of water, rushing purposefully from source to goal. Man is not direct like that, he is not organized like that, he is not efficient like that. If we are to picture man, we do much better to picture him as a slow and ambling river, taking the longest, most circuitous route from here to there. Man is spread out. As he moves along, the various parts of his life interweave, separate and go their different ways, rejoin with whirlpool fury, frustrate and inhibit one another, and only rarely join in a strong and self-defining unity.

So to categorize people is dangerous indeed. But with that warning heard, it may also be useful. For if we are not solely the members of one category or another, we may nonetheless have tendencies or emphases which are worth noticing. If we can see where we fit most comfortably, if we can decide which category describes us most accurately, then we may be able to understand ourselves a bit more fully. And that understanding may just help us in our search for personal holiness.

And so, by way of broadening our reflections on the topic of this book, I would like to suggest that all men can be viewed as falling into one of two groups. A man is either a collector or a creator.

Collectors are those people who spend their lives in the search for some ultimate form of security. Their goal in all things is the safe and the certain.

They may attempt to find their security in money; that is certainly the most blatant example of this group. But collectors may also attempt to achieve their goal through the accumulation of power and influence. Or they may try to use physical isolation, high walls and fences, for protection. The apparently imaginative and innovative search for knowledge may even hide the collector's instinct. Many a scholar has been motivated at one time or another by the conviction that if only he knew enough, if only he conquered ignorance sufficiently, he would eliminate once and for all the fearfulness of life. And for some scholars this conviction is a thoroughgoing principle of life.

And as if this were not enough, even the beauty and wonder of human relationships may become the pawns of the collector. For just as loneliness and personal isolation are among the gravest examples of the insecurity of life, so the relationship of love between two persons is its strongest antidote. And for the collector, this fact may become a grave temptation. His goal is to achieve relationship with others at any cost: to earn it, to buy it, to beg it, to steal it. No matter by what means, relationships must be collected as a bastion against the turmoils of life.

But whatever the object of their acquisitive urge, all collectors are fundamentally the same. They live life out of fear. I am not saying that the collector is different because he has fears in his life. All of us are familiar with fear. No, what makes the collector different is that fear rules his life. The basic shape of his life, the idea that describes it and the thrust that drives it, is fear and nothing else.

As we all know, the feeling of fear is a feeling of emptiness, a void in the middle of the person. And consequently, if we were to imagine a single gesture, a simple movement that would capture the collector in the eye of our mind, that gesture would be one of gathering, of pulling in, of capturing, and of holding. The collector is fundamentally an introjective person. He seeks to take hold of whatever comes near, to make it his own, and to consume it. In some strange, primordial sense, the collector wishes to swallow the world, to take it into himself, in the hopes that once inside of him it will fill the void within. Fear can be forced out only if the person is full. And only collecting can hope to bring that about.

The tragedy of the collector, of course, is that the void is never filled. When we consume the ordinary food of our daily lives, we never succeed in converting all of it to useful nourishment. Always with good there is some waste. And even that part of our food which does nourish us, which fills our needs and assuages our hunger, soon passes. Hunger pangs, thirst, that empty feeling in the stomach, all these inevitably return. And so it is with the collector. The hollow feeling of fear returns. And his hope, his desire, his need remain unfulfilled.

And then there are creators. Creators are people of enthusiasm, of confidence. Creators seem to live with an energy that comes from them rather than going to them. In social situations, in professional and career responsibilities, in recreational activities, in personal relationships, one is preeminently conscious of the creator's contribution. He gives to these situations far more than he receives from them.

The creator exhibits a powerful fertility in his life. His activities and his energies are forever bearing fruit, reduplicating and multiplying themselves. He seems possessed of an almost miraculous power to increase the total quality of life in the world which he inhabits.

A gesture, then, which would characterize the creator for our mind's eye would be one of openness, of trust, and of vivacity. This is not to say that it would be the typical gesture of the extrovert, flamboyant and effervescent. No, the creator is not some sort of super salesman, a hale-fellow-well-met. Those qualities are much more likely to be the thinly disguised ploys of an inveterate collector. The creator, on the other hand, operates out of a genuine and intrinsic enthusiasm, a *joie de vivre* without calculation or guile.

Thus, where the collector fundamentally lives out of fear, the creator lives purely and simply out of love. When he is enthusiastic, he is expressing real affection and respect. When he is gentle, it is because he truly cares. And when he is silent, it is because he is listening. All of these postures, and a thousand more, are but expressions of a profound and perduring love.

Now there is no doubt that if the world is totally divided into collectors and creators, we would all wish to be the latter. But life is not so simple. For despite all the nasty and condemnatory things we can say about collectors, there is a certain virtue to their position. Whether we like it or not, the fact of the matter is that all men do, indeed, need security. Whether we are inclined to readily admit it or not, fear plays a powerful role in the conduct of all our lives. And so the goals of the collector are not, after all, that outrageous. They are reasonable, they are real, they are eminently human. We can sympathize with the collector. And more than that, we can see him in ourselves.

Thus, if we are to break out of our collector's posture and become more and more the creators that we wish to be, we dare not attempt to ignore the fearful and security-seeking aspects of ourselves. Rather we must face those elements of our person and deal with them. Perhaps the message and person of Jesus Christ can help us with that task.

"If anyone comes to me and does not hate his own father and mother and wife and children and brothers and sisters, yes, and even his own life, he cannot be my disciple. Whoever does not bear his own cross and come after me, cannot be my disciple" (Lk. 14:26f). These are the words that Jesus spoke. And they are, to be sure, among the more mysterious and frightening of his words. What can they possibly mean? How can we possibly obey them?

It seems to me that these words from the gospel of Luke are really saying that to be a collector and to be a disciple of Jesus are utterly incompatible. I do not believe that Jesus is inviting us, here, to do active injury to those who are closest to us. He is not suggesting that we despise and insult our relatives. He is not even giving us permission to ignore and disdain them. Given all the other words that Jesus spoke during his ministry and that are recorded for us in scripture, that would be unthinkable. Rather, what he is saying is that we must more and more come to a love for our fellow man that is not possessive, not the love of collectors, but rather a love which is the generous and self-forgetful love of the creator.

We are not, then, in a situation where we *may* forsake the role of the collector on the grounds that we find it distasteful and demeaning. Rather we are in a situation where we *must* turn from that role if we are to be the disciples of Jesus Christ.

But these are not the only words of Jesus. He also said: "I tell you solemnly, there is no one who has left house, wife, brothers, parents or children for the sake of the kingdom of God who will not be given repayment many times over in this present time and, in the world to come, eternal life" (Lk. 18:29f). And here is the other side of the coin. If we are to succeed in overcoming the drive within us to be collectors, we are going to need to have our fears alleviated, our security guaranteed. And in Jesus Christ this comes about. If the presence of God on earth in Jesus means anything, it means that all the hopes and aspirations of man, all the dreams and desires and, yes, needs of man, will be fulfilled. The Christian is, or should be, the most creative of men on this earth. And he is able to be this precisely because he is the most secure and the most fearless of men.

In this passage Jesus promises to reward all of our confidence and trust and unpossessiveness. In other places he has promised to be with us all days, to come again, to be our way, our truth, our life. And all these words, indeed all the actions of Jesus Christ, have this same message throughout:

that man need fear no more, that he need not per-
sist in the foolish search for security. For this has
already been given to him.

Here, then, lies the real irony of collectors and
creators. The collector is by definition the man
who does not have those things which he most
deeply and most intensely desires. He is truly the
poor man, and he proves his poverty by the very
intensity of his search. The creator, on the contrary, is not the man who does not have these
same needs and aspirations. Rather, he is the man
who by some stroke of luck or miracle of grace
already possesses the very things the collector
seeks.

For this reason, above all others, the Christian
must be a creator. We have the collector's need
to overcome our fear, to find security and peace in
our lives. But precisely because we have these
realities as gifts from Jesus Christ, we are spared
the torture of the collector's endless search for
them. Because we are rich in the gifts of Christ we
are free. And because we are free we are able to
be genuinely and profoundly creative.

The man who is empty must live out of fear.
But the man who is gifted with riches can live out
of love. And that is why Jesus never tells us
simply to love one another. Rather he always calls
us to love one another as he has loved us. Because

we have received all the things we need most deeply as gift, we now can and must share the life within us in a response of thoroughgoing love.

When we took mathematics in school, we were all taught that two plus two equals four. That may be true in mathematics, but in life it is different. For the collector, sad as he is, two plus two equals three. Somehow he always ends up with less than he expects. He never quite achieves the goal he seeks, the goal that should be commensurate with his efforts.

And on the contrary, for the creator two plus two equals five. In his liveliness, in his generosity, in the openness and sincerity of his love, the creator always seems to end up with more than he should. He increases the quantity and quality of life, the warmth and beauty of the world in which he lives. And if he is able to effect this miracle of creation, it is because of the divine power of the gift out of which he lives. And that gift is Jesus Christ.

Whether to be a collector or a creator, that is a clear question for us. For in life, unlike mathematics, one thing is for sure. Two plus two never equals merely four.

Chapter Seven

BLOCKS

Can you imagine yourself writing a book on the topic of personal holiness? Or, at least, can you imagine yourself writing such a book with total confidence, with full security, and with no hesitation? I imagine that you cannot—and neither can I. When I first undertook to express my ideas on this topic I knew full well my own uncertainties and hesitations. I knew the doubts that I had regarding my own competence, indeed regarding the propriety of my writing this book.

But what struck me in an amused and somewhat embarrassed way was the fact that those who are close to me agreed with me! "Oh really," they said, "and what gives you the right to compose that book? Do you really know what holiness is? Have you really achieved personal holiness to the point where you can tell others about it?"

That was what people said, and they only reinforced my own feelings.

It is one of the strange facts of our faith that while theologians declare holiness to be the normal state of the Christian, none of us genuinely feels that he or she has achieved that state. St. Paul regularly refers to the Christians to whom his letters are written as "the saints." But I am sure there are precious few Christians today who would be comfortable with that title. We all feel so far from the ideal which we envision for ourselves. We are all so intensely conscious of our weaknesses, our failings, our sins. We all see so clearly the inadequate character of our commitment to Jesus Christ and to his gospel.

Of course, some of this self-criticism is more neurotic than appropriate. To some extent each one of us is the captive of that Jansenist obsession with the worthlessness of the self. And to the extent that this is the case we must all wage a perpetual battle against the temptation to denigrate ourselves.

But to some extent this self-understanding is not neurotic; it is true. To some extent or other, each and every one of us is genuinely deserving of the criticism we level. To say that we are less than we ought to be, to concede that we have not embraced the good news of Jesus Christ to the extent that we should, to say this is simply to say the truth. So one of the questions we must certainly address in our reflections on the topic of personal holiness is the simple question of why this is so. Why are we less than perfect? Why do we fail to meet our own ideals? Why do we continue to fall short of the mark we have set for ourselves, and that God has set for us?

The title of this meditation refers to at least a partial answer to those questions. For it seems to me that there are a number of blocks to our growth in personal holiness, to our development in the Christian life. And to ignore these blocks is simply to be unrealistic.

The blocks that I see, and that I will consider in this meditation, can all be summarized in one generic term. But it is a term which, because of its history, I am very hesitant to use. That term is original sin. For so many of us the notion of original sin is inescapably tied up with apples and serpents, with the Garden of Eden and the Tree of Knowledge, with Adam and Eve who lived so long ago. And consequently that notion has become practically useless for us in our understanding of our Christian lives. So let us speak not of original sin, but of blocks to personal holiness. And let us consider together some of the blocks which stand in our way.

First of all, I find in myself, and I see in other men, an apparently perennial temptation to be "co-opted." This term came into vogue in the 1960s as part of the jargon of the radical left. They used it to describe the incredible capacity of "the establishment" to buy off its critics, to distract them from their mission, and by giving them "a piece of the action" to seduce them into becoming establishment themselves. But it seems to me that the term refers with equal justice, and perhaps more, to a general temptation in the life of every man.

I don't know if social scientists have ever proved the fact, but my own experience suggests to me that in the long run any group tends to assume as its posture the lowest common denominator of its members. When I am in a group I, too, tend to behave as the group expects. No matter what my ideals, no matter what the vision I fabricate for myself in isolation, in the presence of others I am often enough co-opted. Of course this co-opting *can* work in both directions. That is, the presence of others may call forth in me behavior better than I demand of myself. If the group has already adopted standards for itself, I may very well be seduced into adopting those same standards myself. But that series of events, sad to say, is much less common. Generally speaking, I am co-opted down, not up.

Beyond this, however, there is another sense in which the tendency to be co-opted stands as a block to personal holiness. I am thinking of the strange way groups have of subtly and unconsciously pre-defining the limits of their concern. And connected to this is the equally subtle temptation we all share to accept and subscribe to those limitations.

Let me illustrate what I mean. More often than I care to admit, I have been a member of groups which were genuinely but narrowly Christian in their focus. They might have been groups oriented toward prayer, toward apostolic concern, toward theological reflection, or toward ministry in the Church. But no matter what the orientation, my experience was the same. At one point or another I was profoundly struck by the originality of some particular contribution. Most of us had done nothing but continue to think along the same lines as in the past. We had persisted in retilling the same ground in a useless search for new insight. Then suddenly one of the members approached the topic from a thoroughly fresh viewpoint. He or she asked a genuinely new question, contributed a truly original insight, and thereby pointed us in another, far more worthwhile direction.

The contribution of this participant was, of course, a great blessing. But what particularly struck me was the blindness of the rest of us in not seeing it before. How could we have remained so long within the narrow framework of our focus? How could we have missed the fact that the object of our attention was nothing more than a small, comparatively insignificant aspect of reality? Why did it take us so long to break through the horizons of our attention into the fertility of these new perspectives?

In other words, why were we so thoroughly and so easily co-opted by the collective limitations of our vision? And (another question that follows from this) how often is our growth in personal holiness inhibited and obstructed by this tendency toward being co-opted?

In retrospect it seems to me that one of the major blocks to development in the Christian life is just such a lack of vision. It is not a lack of personal dedication or even a lack of will power. It is simply a lack of the vision necessary to see where we can go. And consequently the challenge of the spiritual life demands that we forego not only settled ways of living, but also settled ways of understanding ourselves, our world, and God.

A second block to the development of personal holiness is not nearly so subtle. Put plainly and simply it is the fickleness of our human nature.

I have given up smoking so many times in my life, I have dedicated myself so regularly to getting up early and to working with efficiency, and I have so often spoken sincere but meaningless promises to keep in touch with departing friends, that I can no longer deny the obvious phenomenon of fickleness. Please understand that I am not talking here about genuine ill will. The focus of my attention is not our perverse inclination to make promises and plans which we know full well we have no intention of keeping. Rather I am considering the very sincere and very goodwilled decisions that we make and then fail to fulfill.

The road to hell, goes the old chestnut, is paved with good intentions. And that cliché is verified in the life of every man. For some strange reason we simply do not have the same intentions at one moment as we do at another. The commitment of today, felt to be of paramount importance, has a strange way of becoming nearly meaningless in the midst of the new challenges of tomorrow. There is within each one of us an indecisiveness, a changeableness, a real and profound fickleness that makes us undependable even to ourselves.

If we were to conjure up an image to describe the human person, I am sure most of us would wish to select images that convey some solidness. We might say that man is like a tree growing toward the sky. Or we might envision man as part of the good earth, as American Indians do. But as much as I hate to admit it to myself, I must confess that man seems to me to be much more like the clouds above. Man does have some shape, he is not absolutely fluid. But that shape is subject to numberless changes and permutations. And even what shape there is can move from one height to another, from one place to another.

As a man, I would like to be strong and solid. But often enough I find myself to be fluid and shifting. For some strange reason I lack a grasp on myself, an ability to take myself and make of myself some one particular thing. I am many things to myself at different times and in different situations. Despite my good intentions there lies a fickleness within me. And this fickleness, it cannot be denied, is a serious block to my growth in personal holiness.

Our fickleness does not extend to every moment and every situation, of course. There are people who have persevered in their intention to quit smoking. If the current proliferation of dieting groups bears witness to the fickleness of which I have been talking, it also bears witness to the perseverence of some members in overcoming that fickleness. But this fact simply leads me to the third block to growth in personal holiness.

Immediately on the other side of fickleness there stands another wall to our personal development, a wall that I experience in myself and see in others. Particularly in the more explicitly spiritual dimensions of our lives, I find a recurring temptation to continue certain forms of behavior while losing the underlying reason for those forms. I call this temptation "surfacing out."

Perhaps you can recall the experience of Lenten resolutions. On Ash Wednesday a serious commitment is made to attend daily Mass, say, or to abstain from the evening cocktail. And what is more, this resolution is made for some serious and spiritual reasons. Because I wish to come closer to God I will give the time for daily worship. Because I wish to participate in the sufferings of our Savior I will deny myself one of the comforts of my life. And for some days or weeks both the behavior and the reason remain closely joined in my inner decision.

But sooner or later, I suddenly notice that a frightening change has taken place. True, I am still doing the action to which I committed myself. I have not given in to the temptation of fickleness. But at some quiet, unnoticed moment I have lost the inner reason for what I do. Suddenly I find that I am attending daily Mass primarily in order to satisfy my own pride. I wish to be able to say on Easter morning that I have "not missed a day." Or I discover that the genuine reason why I continue to abstain from that cocktail is that I have found it a relatively easy way to lose those five excess pounds. In some unexplainable way and at some unremembered moment I have lost the connection between inner spiritual motivation and outer action. I have become a legalist, in the true and humiliating sense of that word. I have fallen victim to what T. S. Eliot has called the greatest sin:

to do the right thing for the wrong reason. In a word, I have surfaced-out.

No matter how difficult it is to adopt and maintain truly Christian forms of behavior, that accomplishment is not the most difficult of all. Far more difficult is the adoption and maintenance of a truly Christian motivation. Indeed, it has been suggested that the noon-day devil of the Christian life is the temptation to lose the inner man while preserving the shell of virtuous action. In the heat of the sun it is all one can do to continue to act in a proper way. The cultivation and enrichment of core commitment is simply more than one can muster.

And so, because it is my own experience and because I see it so often in others, I suggest that the perversely inevitable tendency to surface-out is one of the major blocks to personal holiness.

But beneath the human propensities to be co-opted, to be fickle and to surface-out lies the deepest and most insidious block of all. It is difficult to find the proper name for this block, but it is very easy to describe its feeling. It is a certain fearfulness, an anxiousness that prompts hesitancy about all we do. It is that apprehension which results from our awareness of the risk-element that is part of all our actions and commitments. It is the "free floating anxiety" of the psychologists and the *angst* of the existentialists. And it is very much related to the "Not OK Child" of Transactional

Analysis. For myself, because the feeling bears so much resemblance to acrophobia, the fear of heights, I would like to call this block cosmic acrophobia.

It is the sense of not being in complete control of our lives. We all try so hard to control our activities, to direct our destinies, to be completely in charge of our lives. We organize our day, we plan our year. We schedule our appointments and rehearse our major activities. And yet despite the care that we take, we know in our hearts that "anything may happen."

Indeed, not only is it possible that outside circumstances may intrude upon my plans and obstruct them, it is also true, and far more disturbing, that I may end up being the intruding force myself. Not only am I unsure of what others may do, I am unsure of what I may do. The hold I have upon myself, upon my hopes and aspirations, is tenuous indeed. And while my past actions give me some probability about my future decisions, the simple fact is that I am not absolutely sure what I might do in any particular circumstance. It is not so much that some "thing" outside of me is out of my control, but rather that I am out of my control. And so all my actions, all my intentions and plans, are suffused with the pain of cosmic acrophobia.

My place on the evolutionary ladder is high

indeed, and the air up here is exceedingly thin. The demands at this level for free decision and self-direction are perhaps more than I can handle. The cosmic heights on which I find myself, and all men find themselves, are more than a little dizzying. And it is hard to catch one's breath.

The result of all this, then, is like the result of regular acrophobia. In the clutches of one's fear a certain paralysis sets in, an inability to act at all. Or at the very least, each individual movement is invested with a care and calculation which is debilitating and ultimately frustrating. That smooth and confident ease which should characterize the actions of the mature human being is disrupted, and it is replaced by a devastating hesitation.

Isn't this the case in so much of our Christian lives? Where one would expect a firm and enthusiastic stride in the direction of justice or charity or altruism, one discovers instead a hesitancy to take any risks at all. And instead of a willing and joyful dependence on the gifts of a loving God, one finds a continual attempt to "hedge our bets."

Once again, as in the other blocks we have considered, there is no question here of ill will. Cosmic acrophobia is not the burden of the selfish and uncommitted person. Quite the contrary, it is the perennial cross of the very man or woman who seeks to follow Christ. And just as the neurotic fear of heights cannot be exorcised by any amount of rationalization, so cosmic acrophobia continues to exert its influence despite the best of intentions. It is, when all is said and done, an apparently perennial block to growth in personal holiness.

Being co-opted, fickleness, surfacing-out, and cosmic acrophobia: these are the blocks which I have noted and considered at some length. But in considering them I have done little more than tender a loose description. I have come nowhere near explaining these blocks or offering any suggestions for the future. Is there anything I can say about these four realities, is there any word of understanding or hope that I can offer?

I mentioned at the beginning that all four of these blocks could, if it were not for our stereotypes, be aptly summarized under the traditional notion of original sin. So perhaps by way of conclusion we can discover in that idea some illumination for ourselves.

Traditional theology, of course, viewed original sin as a reality in the life of each and every Christian. It was not viewed as a reality for which the Christian was necessarily responsible. But it was understood as something with which we must all deal whether we like it or not. Original sin is simply a permanent aspect of our world, and no degree of denial can remove it.

It is also a teaching of our faith, to be sure, that original sin is removed by the sacrament of baptism. But even here the picture painted by traditional theology was not altogether encouraging. For that theology stipulated that even with the elimination of original sin itself, the effects of original sin would remain. Such realities of human experience as ignorance, weakness of will, and a certain rebelliousness of sense appetites would continue to plague even the person who had been incorporated into the Body of Christ. And only the coming in power of Jesus at the end of time would dispose of those burdens and grant the Christian the integrity and facility for which he yearns.

These ideas, it seems to me, give us a perspective from which to view the blocks we have been considering. Perhaps, to be accurate, we should consider those blocks not as aspects of original sin itself, but rather as some of those effects of original sin. Be that as it may, the point for our lives is the same. The search for personal holiness in which we are engaged is not an easy or quickly completed thing. Indeed, it is not something that will ever be completed within the limits of this life. The blocks I have been describing in this chapter will never be completely overcome, they will never be utterly eliminated. As long as I attempt to pursue the path to personal holiness, I will have to contend with these tendencies within me. In fact, if I ever find that they are no longer a problem, that will more than likely be an indication that I have forsaken the Christian life altogether.

The blocks to the full expression of the Christian life are not personal sins to be repented and forsaken. Rather they are the unfortunate but very real ambit within which that life is lived. The measure of our personal holiness is not the degree to which we have been freed from these blocks. In fact in the final analysis, perhaps the measure of personal holiness is the degree to which we have accepted them.

And nevertheless persevered.

Chapter Eight

INTERPERSONAL HOLINESS

Several years ago I wrote a book for the same publisher who has brought you this volume (*What A Modern Catholic Believes About Suffering And Evil*). That book contained a dedication that was expressed in four simple letters: R.M.O'C. You may have noticed that this present volume also is dedicated, though in this case the letters are D.H.O'C.

I am sure that the last two letters of each dedication give more than a hint regarding the identities of the persons involved. But I am glad to remove any lingering doubts by admitting that they are my parents, Rosemary McGough and Desmond Henry O'Connell.

I introduce my parents into these meditations not because they were extraordinary people—though to me they were extraordinary indeed. Nor do I mention them because of the colorful character of their lives—though that, too, was noteworthy. And I do not intend to propose them as models of ideal parenthood or outstanding Christianity—though in my biased judgment one could do far worse than to imitate the style of their lives. Rather, I bring them up here for the uncomplicated reason that they were a major influence on my own desire for personal holiness.

In reflecting on my own life, and in discussing with other people their own experiences, I am struck by the fact that holiness, that apparently most personal of all realities, is actually interpersonal in the extreme. And that for a number of reasons.

First of all, personal holiness is interpersonal because it is largely a received reality. In the first chapter of this book I mentioned that holiness is ultimately not a human achievement but rather a divine gift. It is something we freely receive from God. Our only contribution is to be ready for that gift. But now, upon further reflection, we realize that even this readiness is the result of numberless human gifts throughout our lives.

Where did I learn to love? Where did I learn perseverance and patience? What was the source of my conviction that persons and relationships are more important than things and tasks? Each one of us may have different answers to these questions. Some may, like myself, cite their parents as the primary influence. Others may mention relatives, friends, colleagues, or teachers. But I am sure that the *leitmotif* of all our responses will be some other person or persons in our lives.

Indeed, even if the contribution of others was only to portray the opposite of our ideals, that portrayal provided us a real service just the same. In no case did we fabricate out of whole cloth the core convictions and the central vision of our existence. No, these were gifts from others. And inasmuch as these gifts provided us with the capacity for personal holiness, they made that holiness profoundly interpersonal.

Christian holiness is also interpersonal in its many effects. This is a point we carefully noted in the meditation on "Action," and there is no need to repeat all the details here. Suffice it to say that because of man's intrinsically social nature and, just as importantly, because of the social and interpersonal commands of Jesus, holiness requires expression. Genuine Christian holiness must express itself in active concern for and involvement in the lives of others. There is no such thing as isolated holiness, sterile holiness. Those are contradictions in terms.

Personal holiness, then, is interpersonal in a variety of ways. It is interpersonal in its sources, in its effects, and in its very nature.

But why is this? Is there any deeper sense in

which we can understand this fact? Any added insight which can help to illuminate all this? I think there is. And so in this final meditation I would like to share some reflections on the deepest, most ultimate doctrine of our faith: the Trinity. For to my mind the Trinity offers us the most profound perspective from which to appreciate the interpersonal nature of holiness.

Since we were children we have spoken of God as triune. "One God in three persons," those were the words we used. But what do those words really mean? Contemporary theologians like to remind us of ideas about God which have been part of our tradition for centuries. And they like to develop those ideas in order to answer that question.

The Trinity, they say, is not accidentally three persons. For, in some deep sense nothing in God is an accident. God is a "necessary being," and his composition is therefore also in some way "necessary." Thus if we discover that our God is, indeed, comprised of three distinct persons, then this must be so for some necessary and inescapable reason. This is the first idea. And God is an utterly perfect being. God is total existence, infinite reality, without weakness and without limit. That is the second idea. But if these two ideas are true, if God is absolutely perfect and if God is comprised of three necessary persons, then a powerful conclusion faces us.

That conclusion is that perfect existence is fertile existence. It is not existence luxuriating in splendid solitude, but rather existence exploding into fellowship. It is existence reveling in relationship, thriving in the richest of communities. The Trinity as community: that is the theme of today's theologians.

What does this word "community" mean? In our human experience a community is a group of persons bonded together in a unity, a common life. But the common life shared in community is not, or should not be, the sort that swallows the individual, that robs him of his individuality and reduces him to the level of a "member." No, it is or should be the sort that nourishes the individual, makes him more deeply his own, liberates him from and for himself. Community, indeed, is or should be the place where individual human persons find together a variety and a complementary uniqueness that is impossible for anyone alone.

A single common life with cherished uniqueness. Those are the characteristics of community in our world. And shot to infinity they are the characteristics of our God. In the community we call the Trinity, the common life is so real, so thorough, so effective, that in reality we can speak of only one God, not three. And yet in some mysterious way, this common life is so solicitous, so respectful of its components, that we must also speak of three distinct persons.

And what is it that makes these persons different? Here a third idea culled from our traditional theology offers a pregnant answer. It is the unique quality of their specific relationships that makes the persons different. That and nothing more. The Son is in actuality the Father, so the theologians said, in all respects save one: he is the Father's Son. And the Spirit is distinguishable from the Father and the Son in no way at all except that he is, indeed, their Spirit. It is their relationships that give them their uniqueness, just as it is their relationships that make them one.

The point of all this is that we Christians do not only have a personal God, we have an interpersonal God. We have a God who is unity and diversity together, who is community. We have a God who sanctifies relationship in the fact that he is himself constituted by relationship. And this makes all the difference in our understanding of personal holiness.

In the first meditation of this book we defined personal holiness as union with God. Now we realize that it is union with an interpersonal God. It is a strange sort of membership in the divine community. And if our previous conclusions led us to assert that personal holiness is actually interpersonal in its sources, its effects, and its nature, we are no longer the least bit surprised. For personal holiness is nothing less than the presence of an interpersonal God in interpersonal union with the Christian man or woman. Far from being the solipsistic experience we sometimes envision in our caricatures, personal holiness is consummately social in its every aspect. From beginning to end, it is not personal holiness at all. It is interpersonal holiness that we seek.

That is what the Trinity tells us about our topic. That is the illumination it sheds. And now, by way of conclusion, let me add one further insight.

In the first meditation, in the context of developing a definition of personal holiness, we pursued our thoughts into the mysterious reality of love. We saw that holiness is the gift of love because it is the gift of God, and God is love. Now, at the very end, that makes more sense, too. For love is the most interpersonal of all realities, it is the defining characteristic of interpersonal unions. Love is the free bond between persons, and love is the liberating gift of individuality. Love is the very constitutive power of community.

It is because God is love, then, that he is community at all. And it is because God is community that we are offered the gift of holiness. And consequently, the personal holiness which has been this book's topic is not some dry exercise, some ponderously dull religious task. Rather it is a rich, intoxicating, frightening but inviting journey into interpersonal love.

It is love received as gift from a loving God. It is love seeking to look beyond appearances to the deeper mystery. It is love manifesting itself in human sacraments. It is love expressing itself in conscious prayerful union. It is love overflowing in generous action. It is love letting go of itself in creativity. It is love accepting and tolerating the inevitable blocks to its own full enjoyment. Personal holiness is love. And for that reason, above all others, it is interpersonal from start to finish.

But if personal holiness is love, it also shares the character of love. Just as love knows no limits, neither does personal holiness. Like love, personal holiness is not so much a complete and finished object as it is a continuing and developing project. We should probably not speak of love at all, but rather of loving. And thus, in the final analysis, we should reject the abstract idea of holiness in favor of the dynamic project of becoming holy.

To talk about personal, or interpersonal, holiness in this book has been an awkward and frustrating task. The words have been clumsy and the ideas have been rough. And now we finally see why. For in a very real sense our topic does not exist. As man is just coming to be, as love must continue to grow or else die, as community is an ultimately dynamic reality, so holiness in the end is no-thing. Our words fail us because, to tell the truth, words are impotent in the face of personal holiness. And so the "last word" on our topic must be a helpless word, a word of concession, a willing word of silence. . . .

We are on the way to personal holiness, you and I. And we really don't know what it will look like when we're done. All we can do is share our past experiences, point out the future direction that seems best, and offer some encouragement along the way.

After that, we must proceed to live.